We all have presentations to give.

The Prezi
Presentation Paradigm

The Prezi Presentation Paradigm

TESOL Strategy Guide

DAVID KENT

Pedagogy Press

National Library of Australia Cataloguing-in-Publication entry:
Kent, David Bradley, author.
The Prezi presentation paradigm / David Kent.

ISBN: 9781925555059 (paperback) (2)
TESOL strategy guide ; 2.
Includes bibliographical references.
Teachers of English to Speakers of Other Languages.
Prezi (Computer software).
Presentation graphics software.
Educational technology.
English language—Study and teaching—Foreign speakers.

Pedagogy Press. Sydney, Australia.
www.pedagogypress.com

First Edition.

For teachers everywhere.

CONTENTS

Preface

This *TESOL Strategy Guide*, number two in the set, arose out of the clear need to provide teacher training and a means of professional development to educators, living and working in the Republic of Korea. Many expatriate English language instructors have arrived in-country without training as a teacher or educator and are often left to take care of their own professional development while engaged in teaching English to speakers of other languages (TESOL). As many of these teachers come to enjoy working as expatriates, they often begin to seek out their own professional development on topics that they wish to learn more about, on skills that they wish to gain, and on techniques that they wish to integrate within their classrooms. It is this need, which is common to all teachers of English in all contexts around the globe, that this book seeks to fill.

Organization of the text

Each *TESOL Strategy Guide* can be read standalone or in conjunction with others from the set. Each book provides information on a technology topic, and has been designed around a question-based format similar to the following:

- Overview
- What is … ?
- How can I use … ?
- What types of … exist?
- What elements are behind an effective … ?
- How can … lend itself to TESOL?
- How can I start using … with students?
- How do I evaluate a … ?
- What tools are available for … creation?
- How do I craft a … ?
- How would I use a tool to create a … ?
- What are the key points behind … use in the TESOL context?

A comprehensive list of resources with links to pertinent web sites and applications is included, along with lesson plan guides, example implementation techniques, and various free to use handouts for the teacher and student alike. A reference list of all works cited also allows those teachers with an interest in a particular topic to engage in reading further on the issues that most interest them and impact their learners.

It is hoped that this book will provide both education and something new for all teachers – be they trained or untrained, pre-service, in-service, seasoned, or retired.

1

Overview

Every student has, at some point in his or her academic life, been required to give a presentation, and in recent years, class presentations have needed to be tied increasingly to multimedia. It is here where Prezi offers a dynamic means of creating a multimedia-based presentation that can actively engage students, particularly in the smart board context where touch navigation is a key component, and one that allows for carrying out a variety of activities from within the same presentation. Prezi use also promotes active learning, with strengths of the presentation platform providing a unique way to establish interest in key topics, direct attention to various subjects, motivate and engage learners, and draw on the creative talents of students as they start to design and develop their own Prezis. The pedagogical possibilities arising from the use of the Prezi presentation paradigm in the context of teaching English to speakers of other languages (TESOL) are offered, along with an overview of instructional strategies, tasks, and activities suitable for multimedia presentation development with learners. Tutorials on how to get started with Prezi are included, along with photocopiable handouts and templates, evaluation techniques, and a comprehensive resource list.

2
What is Prezi?

With over 30 million presentations made daily (Swinford, 2006), Keynote is one system that people who prefer Apple applications may use, yet the more familiar and perhaps most ubiquitous presentation tool might be the Microsoft solution PowerPoint. Both Keynote and PowerPoint are long standing presentation creation tools developed primarily for the business world, have been used for decades, and have a well-established classroom place and use. On the other hand, Prezi was initially developed by Adam Somlai-Fischer and released to the public in 2009 as a visualization tool with the aim of being intuitive to use, and to develop ideas and disseminate them in the form of a visual narrative that can transition from a big picture perspective to focus on specifics with ease (Lechlitner, Kocain, Reitz, Stroman, Kwon, Sheldon, Peedin, Chalfant, Robinson, Siebenhausen, Towns, Boldebuck, Applegate, Cain, & Cunningham, 2011).

Prezi uses a zoomable user interface (ZUI) that allows users to move around a canvas in both a linear and non-linear fashion. In other words, think of a Prezi as a large whiteboard that allows you to layout ideas, media, and connections, and move between the concepts these objects represent via non-linear transitions (Bruder, 2011). This allows for the emergence of creativity as presenters can essentially walk through a mind map, exploring and focusing upon the ideas emanating from each represented concept, while being free to move or zoom around non-sequentially between any place or part of these constructs (Crosby, 2010). This is in contrast to traditional applications like Keynote and PowerPoint that provide users with an avenue to develop slides that contain printable handouts, or showcase multimedia (audio, graphics, and video) in a single sequential file.

Prezi is available to teachers and students for free, and allows teachers to make Prezis either available publicly, make them private, or share them with select individuals. Public Prezis can be easily disseminated from the Prezi website; links to private Prezis must be emailed to others while other users can be invited to share the Prezi. Sharing a Prezi with others can allow for collaborative learning to occur, with students working in teams of up to ten people to edit the same presentation simultaneously, or to view the same presentation as a group while it is delivered by a presentation leader.

Prezi, like Keynote and PowerPoint, allows users to incorporate text, graphics, audio, video, and other presentation objects such as PDF documents and YouTube videos. Prezi presentations are primarily created and stored online, but they can be downloaded for local presentation. A desktop application is also available by subscription that allows for local development of content where offline construction may prove necessary.

3

How can I use Prezi?

Prezi offers a dynamic means of presentation that can actively engage students, particularly in the smart board context where touch navigation is a key component in technology use. The Prezi workspace allows for development of contextual relationships between objects at a glance, which helps to engage students visually. The non-linear pathway format allows information to be provided in a flow, which engages students mentally by going with the normal thinking process. Grouping, layering, and zooming promote a focus to engage students in a discussion that can in turn promote deeper understanding of content presented.

In the view of Laurillard, Stratfold, Luckin, Plowman & Taylor (2000, p. 2), multimedia environments allow for learner control over navigational pathways with narrative lines only established "from an interactive collaboration between the user and the program". This means that educators need to be aware that learners engaged with learning from Prezi content may come to perceive the presentation as something very different to the expectations of the presenter if they do not follow a presenter established navigational pathway, or if one is not provided for them to follow before engaging in their own exploration of a Prezi as a concept map, particularly since, computer-based instructional variance can be explained by the unique navigational selection of students (Schar, Schluep, & Schierz, 2000).

Nonetheless, the workspace element of Prezi, being a large and flat canvas, allows students to lay out the different elements of their presentation in any arrangement that they desire. These elements can then be tied together by a navigational pathway that allows users to move backwards and forwards around each element in a linear progression if they want to. This kind of canvas layout is great for any student, adult or child, who needs to brainstorm, move elements around, figure out an order, move things again, and maintain flexibility over the final outline of their actual presentation (Leimbach, 2010).

Students are limited in the amount of text that they can type into text boxes, but this can ensure that their ideas are succinct and are more point- then paragraph-oriented. The formatting of backgrounds and choices with color are also limited to only a few, but this in turn sees students focus more on content objects and how these relate to each other over the actual look of their presentation.

As for teachers, the grouping, layering, and zooming functions allow for key points or features to be hidden in the dot of the 'i' or 'j', and in the period at the end of a sentence. Even tiny explanations, definitions or translations can be associated with keywords in the passage, and zoomed in upon as assistance is required. This function can also be applied to images by the use of frames to zoom in to an area of a graphic – asking students predictive type questions, for example – then zoom out to show the entire image. Details of larger images that are easily lost can also be focused upon in this manner. So too, PDF documents or videos can be embedded in presentations to provide examples, or to further offer clarification of points, but videos have been limited to 50 MB in the free version.

4

What type of educational Prezi can be made?

At the elementary school level, Prezi can be used to assist with story sequencing, solar system layout and labeling, or in developing water and plant life cycle storybooks. In secondary education, Prezi can be used to illustrate themes from literature such as *To Kill a Mockingbird* or to present an historical event from World War II. In computer classes, the preparation and comparison of PowerPoint and Prezi application and development can occur. In post-secondary education, students may create a timeline on Prezi based on a novel in a communications class, provide steps in food preparation in culinary arts, or develop a virtual playbook for use by a coach in sports (Lechlitner et al., 2011). Pinto Pires (2010) also highlights a number of educational uses for Prezi which include displaying a biography-based timeline by creating paths from dates to life event descriptions, by zooming from place to place on a map during geography lessons to provide details and facts about areas, and displaying historical information of a place or person by date and then zooming into the associated facts and details so that they can be reviewed.

5

What elements are behind an effective Prezi?

The key to creating an effective Prezi is in the development of grouping and layering of objects and concepts.

1. Deal with one concept at a time, and cluster content that is connected contextually.
2. Use images over text, as they can represent the essence of the idea that you are trying to convey and are visible when zoomed out.
3. Let your voice be the text of the Prezi, either live while presenting, or by a recorded narration.

Clark (2011) also reminds us to consider the entire canvas as conveying meaning, and suggests using the canvas to create concept maps. He also mentions wrapping the Prezi around a story or metaphor to provide a creative framework to assist students in internalizing concepts. Another suggestion is to provide increased interactivity to engage students in the presentation by integrating participatory activities, such as Poll Everywhere, so that students can provide their own input into an ongoing presentation.

Remember that the point of a presentation is to provide clear communication of information. Outline the Prezi presentation beforehand (perhaps using some other mind map software, or even type up an outline in point form in a word processor), and of course stay in control. Keep the content and size of the Prezi manageable in terms of presentation length, grouping, layering, and navigation choices. Ultimately, to give a flawless presentation, practice the presentation somewhere else beforehand and keep an offline backup for contingency purposes.

6

How can a Prezi lend itself to TESOL?

Educators working in countries where a visual learning style predominates can use Prezi to great effect in the English as a foreign language (EFL) context. The tool can also be used to establish interest in key topics, direct attention to various subjects, motivate and engage learners, and draw on the creative talent of students as they start designing and developing their own Prezis. Students can develop skills associated with mind map development, demonstrate their linguistic level, and reinforce their learning while practicing the language skills that they have already fostered to date.

Prezi has also been used to improve student vocabulary in the secondary school EFL context (Aljehani, 2015), and is recognized by Robinson (2014), along with Peridore and Lines (2011), as the kind of tool that provides learner engagement in the English language arts (ELA) and EFL classrooms by bringing written lectures to life.

However, in and of itself, Prezi will not improve student learning. It requires strategic employment of Prezi to create opportunities for active learning, and to capitalize on the strengths of the presentation platform to engage students in the learning process. Further, as Prezi provides a platform for incorporating a variety of different kinds of multimedia file types, each 'slide' can be multimodal and allow students to demonstrate their understanding and knowledge of learning content in their own unique way, fitting with multiple intelligence and multiple ways of learning (Rhinehart Neas, 2012).

7

How can I start using the Prezi presentation paradigm with students?

As Prezi enables educators with the ability to provide students with a presentation, it can be used in the TESOL classroom just as any other presentation software is used. The Prezi focus can be teacher-centered, student-centered, or a mix of both depending on the use of the editor and on the aim of the lesson being taught. The benefit of Prezi use is that it can contain all the needed components and resources required of a single lesson in one presentation.

In a teacher-centered process, Prezi can be used to enrich existing text-based (or even other internet-based) material, from practice tasks through to language games. A number of traditional EFL classroom activities can also easily transfer to the Prezi setting. For example: teaching new ideas and concepts at the start of a chapter or topic, reviewing vocabulary through practice and drill tasks or quizzes, and providing review material.

In a student-centered process, Prezi work on a topic can be undertaken individually or collaboratively. During the collaboration process, students' speaking and listening skills can improve during concept development and design discussions, while their reading and writing skills can improve during presentation construction. Students can design presentations on any topic from food to fashion. These presentations can be assigned to individuals or as collaborative group work, with each individually created or group created Prezi later coming together as a part of a larger class Prezi. In this manner, each group or individual student would be responsible for completing a single node, or concept, that would come to form part of a larger class Prezi presentation which can be given in class or be archived for later topic review.

Other uses of Prezi in the EFL classroom may include teaching phonics, grammar, vocabulary, writing, and storytelling. Students could also use the tool to complete comparison and retelling tasks, and develop poster projects. Sabio (2010) provides a range of Prezis for teacher reuse, from writing (such as introductory paragraphs, types of sentences, descriptive writing) to speaking (for example, phrasal verbs, relative clauses, quantifiers).

Meanwhile, Prezi for Education is the Prezi educational community home, and offers discounts to educators upgrading from their free account. Also available is the Prezi Education Blog, where posts showcase the use of Prezi in the education context.

8

How do I evaluate a Prezi?

Prezi presentations can be evaluated just like any other (including those provided by Keynote or PowerPoint) through the use of prefabricated rubrics like the example to soon follow. In this case, several overall constructs are being assessed that include:

- presentation of the problem being discussed,
- the background information provided,
- the design and content of the presentation itself,
- resolution of the problem presented, and
- actual oral presentation skills.

As always, rubrics should be provided to learners beforehand so that they understand what will actually be assessed, and can ask questions if they don't understand.

Although it is useful for the busy teacher to apply pre-made rubrics, it is even better if teachers formulate ones of their own which can reflect their teaching environment and the points they wish to assess. One good source for this is Rubistar, where there are a number of premade evaluation options as well as information on how to create unique context-sensitive evaluation instruments. The rubrics section of the resources list also contains several other rubric creation tools that may prove worthwhile to look over.

The rating scale used in the following rubric goes from 1 to 5, with 1 being poor, 2 fair, 3 average, 4 good, and 5 excellent. 'Average' is used as a midpoint so that students can see how each particular skill relates to peers. This allows teachers to identify those skills that are weak in individual students, and those that may need improvement.

Assessment Item	Assessment Criteria	Score
Problem Introduction	Sufficient information is provided, and presented clearly.	1 2 3 4 5
Background Information	Sufficient information is provided, and relevant.	1 2 3 4 5
Content and Design	Too much or too little information per slide; animations, colors, font size, and sounds are appropriate.	1 2 3 4 5
Problem Resolution	Logical progression of argument with facts supporting the solution.	1 2 3 4 5
Oral Presentation Skills	Speakers clearly understand the content, and aim the presentation at the audience (in terms of vocabulary use, rate of speech, and so on).	1 2 3 4 5

Ratings: 1 Poor 2 Fair 3 Average 4 Good 5 Excellent

9

How do I get started with Prezi development?

Although the blank canvas and non-linear presentation style of a Prezi can be empowering, it can also be debilitating for first time users, including students, who may need a lot of guidance in getting started. Further dangers include creating mega-maps that house an overwhelming amount of data, and going overboard with zoom transitions (or jump cuts) from topic to topic, which leads to panning that can cause a form of motion sickness amongst the audience (Leberecht, 2009). Working with a Prezi involves being able to develop a concept map, or mind map, of your project as well as working with a canvas and moving from a big picture view of elements down and through a more detailed and layered structural representation of ideas. This may prove quite challenging for students if they approach Prezi creation in the way they would create a linear Keynote or PowerPoint slide.

Potter (2011) has established several guidelines to assist with initial Prezi development, and a few of these are:

Structure first, detail later

Outline your presentation, determine what the big picture top-down view of the canvas will look like and make this draw in viewer attention, while simultaneously serving to function in support of the presentation subject matter.

Make group sections large

The Prezi canvas is essentially unlimited in size, and everything is zoomed in to fill the presentation frame as required. This means that you can lay out objects over a wide area, with no need to later cram everything in next to each other or have to waste time moving lots of objects around just to fit one more in.

Select themes early

Choose a theme that best suits your presentation and stick with it from the start. This is so that fonts on titles and text in parts of the Prezi presentation will be uniform, and will always stay where you position them and what you position them within.

Avoid transition overuse

Move progressively and consistently between items rather than wildly oscillating around the canvas, zooming in here, out there, and in again somewhere else. Remember, even though the presentation medium may provide you with lots of eye candy, only use additions to your presentation that add value to the content that you present. For example, Prezi can go really big and really small and this can be used to advantage by zooming in on something that a user may not guess is there from the initial top-down view.

Use a uniform style

After establishing the sizes that you want for titles and text in various sections of your Prezi, use the duplicate and edit functions to ensure that all other titles and text are of the same sizes and fonts. Keep in mind that every image used will fill the presentation window, so they must be large and crisp in their native sizes. By the same token, use frames to advantage by setting an invisible frame around groups of objects or small images, as it is the frame that takes the focus and comes to fill the presentation window when Prezi zooms in on it. Also, rely on the quick keys when working with Prezi; for example, holding shift functions to move groups of objects at one time while keeping their spatial relationship intact. Finally, either embed a YouTube video so that it will automatically play or, alternatively, add the video URL as free text and click on it to play it only as required.

10

How do I work with a zoomable user interface?

The key to understanding and working with a zoomable user interface (ZUI) is to completely comprehend the relationship between the conceptual objects that you are placing on the Prezi workspace or canvas and the ways in which these ideas will be linked both hierarchically (in terms of magnification layers) as well by group (in terms of providing a navigational pathway between and among each object and group). To begin with, blocks of content need to be arranged contextually in relation to each other, as users will zoom from one block to another, and down within these blocks to see more detailed views at different levels of magnification. Each block of content can hold several layers of magnification, and this means that a user can zoom into one block from a big picture view showing several blocks, then zoom into an image within the magnified block (filling the presentation frame), and then zoom further down into that image to another object such as piece of text (a YouTube video, a PDF document, or simply a more specific detail of the original image), whose view once again comes to fill the entire presentation frame. The opportunity that these presentation options provide, as Watrall (2009) describes, goes beyond presenting content as chunks strung together in a linear fashion. They provide access to content in a more logically related manner by presenting sets and subsets that are connected spatially and can be navigated non-linearly as well as linearly.

11

How would I create and house a Prezi?

The Prezi website offers very simple and detailed getting-started tutorials which are all very succinct and comprehensive. If you choose to get started straight away, the directions below can help you gain a brief overview of Prezi development before signing up and creating your own account.

Step One – Write

In a Prezi, the entire canvas is the presentation workspace. To get started, simply double-click anywhere on the canvas, and a text box will appear where you can type in a key idea. Ideas can be placed anywhere and dragged around the canvas if more space is required. The canvas is essentially an infinite workspace.

Step Two – Zoom

After adding text-based ideas to the canvas, the zoom feature of Prezi can be used to focus on each of these ideas and allow you to add more text to develop them further. Additional text can be placed anywhere on the canvas at any zoom magnification level. Magnifier buttons are available from the right side menu, or the mouse wheel can be used to zoom in and out of the Prezi.

Step Three – Border menus and text boxes

After clicking on a text box, a menu appears, and it can be used to control several attributes of the object that you have clicked on. The various menus at the top and to the left and right of the Prezi canvas will allow you to arrange all of the text ideas, and establish levels of hierarchy through manipulation of size and placement on the canvas.

Step Four – Importing images

Adding images to the Prezi is controlled from the top menu. Simply click 'Insert' and then 'Image' to locate a local file for import, and after an image appears on the canvas, click on it to activate a menu that controls the placement, size, or other attributes of the image as desired. Prezi development will be faster and smoother if all the images that you wish to use for the Prezi are already collated in a single folder.

Step Five – Develop a presentation narrative

Once all the text and images (along with other files that you may want to use, such as PDF documents or YouTube videos) are arranged in your Prezi, a navigation pathway or a view path can then be chosen. Use the magnifier buttons or mouse wheel to zoom out to look at the entire canvas, as viewing the 'big picture' can assist in establishing the right view path for the Prezi. Click on 'Edit path', then develop your navigational pathway by clicking on each object in the order that you want them to be shown. The order can be changed at any time by dragging an unassigned path ball (the one that appears between path numbers) onto an object, or by dragging a path number away from an object to a blank space on the canvas. It is often a good idea to start out with some meaningful imagery that can be traced or woven through when finalizing the view path.

Step Six – Present and share the Prezi

Clicking on 'Present' moves the Prezi into presentation mode. You can then step forward or backward through the Prezi using the arrow buttons or keyboard arrow keys. In 'Show' mode, you can zoom in or out from each object or you can freely move around the canvas, and a click on the arrow button will return the presentation to the preset navigational pathway. If desired, you can click the 'Share' icon to invite others to view or edit the Prezi, or to obtain an embed code for use with a blog, Moodle, or other web page. The Prezi can also be shared to social media, or it can be downloaded as a PDF document or as a portable Prezi under this icon. The presentation itself will always be housed under your account on the Prezi website, and it will be accessible to you from any web browser.

To assist in getting started with students, a number of photocopiable handouts, including a practice exercise and tutorial, are available in Chapter 14.

12

What are the key points behind Prezi use in the TESOL context?

A number of points to bear in mind while deploying Prezi with students are:

- Prezi uses a zoomable user interface (ZUI) that presents sets and subsets of information that is connected spatially, and can be navigated both non-linearly as well as linearly.

- The Prezi workspace allows for development of contextual relationships between objects at a glance, helping to engage students visually.

- The non-linear pathway format of Prezi presentations allows information to be provided in a flow that engages students mentally by going with the normal thinking process.

- Grouping, layering, and zooming promote a focus to engage students in a discussion which can in turn promote deeper understanding of the relationships that exist amongst the content being presented.

- Students following their own narrative line to explore a Prezi as a concept map may perceive the presentation as something very different to the expectations of the presenter, and this needs to be kept in mind when students use Prezi presentations on their own for learning.

- While sharing and working collaboratively on Prezi development, students' speaking and listening skills can improve during concept development and design discussions, while their reading and writing skills can improve during presentation construction.

- Working with a ZUI requires a good comprehension of the relationship between conceptual objects placed on the workspace and the ways that these will be linked both hierarchically as well as by group.

- Stay in control. Keep the size and content of the Prezi manageable in terms of presentation length, grouping, layering, transition use, and navigation choices.

Software applications like Keynote and PowerPoint may still have their place in the classroom today, but Prezi affords educators and learners an alternative presentation platform. Such a tool offers a dynamic means of presentation, and presentation collaboration, that can engage learners and keep their focus in ever increasing visually oriented touch-driven teaching and technology environments.

13

Lesson plan guides, and example implementation

Provided here are lesson plan guides, focusing on the use and construction of a Prezi, as well an example for implementing Prezi in the educational context. The guides are meant to assist in understanding how to develop a detailed lesson plan, and to help describe what each component and stage of a lesson may cover. The example implementation is intended to provide a use-case scenario detailing the techniques required to apply the use of Prezi in a real-world setting.

The content covered here includes:

- Lesson plan general guide
- Lesson plan guide for Prezi in-class creation and development
- Example implementation: Prezi presentation

Lesson Plan General Guide	
Teaching Context	
Level of Proficiency and Maturity	Student language level (e.g. beginner, intermediate, advanced). Student age range (e.g. young learners, adults).
Lesson Length	Time allotted for the class (e.g. 35-45 minutes).
Lesson Topic	Major theme or focus of the lesson (e.g. numbers and time).
Objectives	Lesson aims (e.g. to teach students how to tell the time and date accurately).
Outcomes	Learning outcomes (e.g. students will be able to read analog and digital timepieces).
Relevant Prior Learning	Anything that students need to know before starting work on this lesson's content (e.g. students need to have completed Chapter Two of the book, and have previously met language associated with appointments, calendars, and timekeeping).

Teacher Preparation	
Hardware	Types of computer or peripherals required (e.g. USB sticks, MP3 players).
Software	Name of software used (e.g. Photo Story 3, Microsoft Word).
Webpage Links	Hyperlink to web resources (e.g. www.google.com).
Additional Resources	Other necessary materials for the lesson (e.g. handouts, worksheets, textbooks).

Procedure			
Stage and Timing	Objective	Teacher	Students
Review Stage (if required, 5 minutes)	Focus of stage (e.g. encourage the use of previously acquired language).	Indicate what the teacher says and does in each stage of the lesson.	Provide expected examples of student behavior.

Warm-up Stage/Pre-Technology Use (10 minutes)	Focus of stage (e.g. introduce new concepts and language to students in a meaningful manner).	Indicate what the teacher says and does in each stage of the lesson.	Provide examples of student comments and behavior.
Main Stage/ Technology-based Activity (20 minutes)	Focus of stage (e.g. allow students to utilize technology to become familiar with and apply the concepts and language content introduced in the lesson).	Indicate what the teacher says and does in each stage of the lesson.	Provide expected examples of student behavior.

Practice Stage (15 minutes)	Focus of stage (e.g. allow learners to utilize the skills and language that they are expected to acquire during the lesson in a practical way).	Indicate what the teacher says and does in each stage of the lesson.	Provide examples of student comments and behavior.
Lesson Summation Stage/Post-Technology Activities (10 minutes)	Focus of stage (e.g. instructor reinforces the importance of language concepts and skills acquired, stating how they will be useful in forthcoming lessons).	Indicate what the teacher says and does in each stage of the lesson.	Provide expected examples of student behavior.

Further Considerations	
Follow-Up Activities	Prepare material that can be applied in a follow up class. Also, be ready with activities for students who complete their class work earlier than expected.
Contingency Plan(s)	Always prepare an alternate teaching scenario in case of any problems. For example, a sudden power outage, or a timetabling issue could make the assigned room unavailable.
Evaluation	Reflect on what worked well, and what did not, and how you might deliver the lesson differently or improve upon it when running it again.

Lesson Plan Guide for Prezi In-Class Creation and Development	
Teaching Context	
Level of Proficiency and Maturity	Beginner to advanced. Adaptable for use with young learners through to adults.
Lesson Length	Several lessons (over a week to a term). Homework completion components. Time allotted for each class: 50 minutes.
Lesson Topic	Variable, from portfolio compilation to single topic presentation.
Objectives	1. Enhance communication skills by expressing opinions on a topic, developing presentation skills, and writing for an audience. 2. Strengthen media literacy and digital literacy skills (use software, images, audio, video, and other media elements or components).
Outcomes	1. Students will create a multimedia-based presentation. 2. Students will employ a range of media resources during their presentation. 3. Students will show evidence of the ability to express personal opinions on a topic.
Relevant Prior Learning	Students will need to be familiar with mind mapping.

Teacher Preparation	
Hardware	Computer or tablet, with internet access and microphone, camera, and scanner (if scanning resources). USB sticks or Google Drive for storage of resources if needed.
Software	Microsoft Word (if mind mapping and note-taking). Prezi.
Webpage Links	Prezi, Flickr, Google image search, freemusicarchive.org.
Additional Resources	Prezi Presentation Preparation handout for students to complete offline, and to work on in class.

Procedure – Day 1 of 2			
Stage and Timing	**Objective**	**Teacher**	**Students**
Review Stage (10 minutes)	Remind students of the elements that make a good presentation. Reintroduce the concept of mind mapping and note-taking for developing a presentation topic.	Teacher elicits information from students by asking questions (e.g. what makes a good presentation? How do you make a mind map?) with responses to be written on the board.	Students should be able to provide several examples of how to give a presentation, and describe the process of how to create a mind map.
Warm-up Stage/Pre-Technology Use (15 minutes)	Introduce the Prezi presentation paradigm.	Show at least one example Prezi as a best practice model.	Students are introduced to a few sample Prezis.

Main Stage (15 minutes)	Develop an initial Prezi with students using the Prezi practice exercise and tutorial handout.	Work through the handout with students, helping them to develop their first Prezi. Introduce new vocabulary as required.	Students work with the teacher, and together, develop an initial Prezi.
Lesson Summation Stage/Post-Technology Activities (10 minutes)	Students should be reminded of the lesson goals, and can be invited to select and show important components of a Prezi, and illustrate the view path.	Remind students of what they should have achieved, help them identify key elements of a Prezi, and ask them to gather resources and a topic idea to create a Prezi of their own for homework.	Students should have a good understanding of the workings of a Prezi, and be able to use the Prezi presentation preparation handout to help them develop an initial outline for a Prezi topic.

Procedure – Day 2 of 2			
Stage and Timing	Objective	Teacher	Students
Review Stage (10 minutes)	Remind students of their homework, and check that it has been adequately completed.	Teacher ensures that an outline of a Prezi presentation has been developed with an associated view path, and that it can be presented in the chosen time frame.	Students have prepared an initial outline and rudimentary view path for their presentation using the homework handout.
Warm-up Stage/Pre-Technology Use (10 minutes)	Elements of presenting and associated vocabulary need to be introduced to students.	The teacher ensures that students understand how to give a presentation, and are aware of the importance of aspects such as body language and voice projection.	Students come to understand that they are the focal point of the presentation, and that the Prezi provides multimedia-based support for their presentation.

Main Stage (20 minutes)	Students use the Prezi presentation preparation handout to finalize their presentation topic.	The teacher assists students in the development of student Prezis, as well as in the writing of any accompanying presentation material.	Students successfully sequence their view path, place their resources, and create matching notes.
Lesson Summation Stage/Post-Technology Activities (10 minutes)	Students should have completed their Prezi development, and be able to export or share it. Otherwise, they will need to complete this task for homework.	Ensures that students have successfully saved or exported a complete Prezi (or are able to do so for homework).	Students complete their Prezi, and produce associated notes to speak along with the presentation. The Prezi should also be exported or saved to share with peers and other stakeholders (e.g. parents).

Further Considerations	
Follow-Up Activities	Students present their Prezi to peers in a following lesson. To do this, students implement the methods that they have been taught to rely on when giving a presentation (for example, using body language and voice projection), and be provided with an appropriate rubric if the Prezi presentation is to be assessed. Audience members should be prepared to ask one question of the presenter.
Contingency Plan(s)	The handout used in the lesson summation post-technology activity can be extended, and used to fill a full class hour. However, if this is not used at this time, then the next lesson in the course syllabus should be ready in case there is a problem with using the Prezi website or other technology. Alternatively, some language games can be prepared to fill in the time if technological problems occur.
Evaluation	What are the biggest frustrations for implementation? Can these be remedied next time? What are the successes of the lesson? What did students get out of this activity? Can more language practice be provided?

Example Implementation:
Prezi Presentation

The Teaching and Learning Context

Prezi can be applied by any teacher who requires their students to develop a multimedia-based presentation. It could be associated with language point reviews with younger learners (for example, presenting idioms and their meanings), the results of collaborative projects with older learners (for example, presenting a demonstration or tutorial), or even job roles when used with adult students (for example, presenting the work-related life of a bank teller). As such, the method of implementation would be well suited for any school, subject, or grade-level. Suitability for use with second-language learners is dependent only upon the teacher's ability to adapt the material to the teaching and learning context, which means that you should ensure that the topic is relevant to both the students' needs and interests.

Teaching Material

The teaching material required can be broken down under three headings: the software, the hardware, and a variety of media resources that students have chosen to use throughout their presentation as learning content.

The software

The Prezi presentation software will be required. It is browser-based, and will need to be used while connected to the internet. Its application for a range of devices can also be downloaded to view and to show a Prezi as required.

The hardware

The minimum hardware required is a device that can access the internet using a web browser, but a built-in microphone may be necessary if students want to record themselves. You will also need a scanner if students wish to scan in samples of their own work, or other offline material, for digitalization.

Learning content

Learning content will stem from students developing a Prezi presentation that comes to revolve around the incorporation of various multimedia elements. These elements could possibly consist of a variety of media, from videos and photographs taken on smartphones to hand-drawn images, and from student-recorded voice through to copyright-free music. The content can already be in a digital format, or it might need to be digitalized.

Procedure

A Prezi presentation can be given and graded, much like any other, such as one that uses Microsoft PowerPoint or Apple Keynote. However, providing a Prezi presentation outline that students can use to help build their own Prezi presentation is perhaps one of the best ways to incorporate the use of the Prezi presentation paradigm in your classes. Why? Because you will be able to provide a tutorial in the use of the software while simultaneously introducing students to the steps that they will need to conduct to complete the presentation task satisfactorily. It will also provide second-language learners with additional language practice as you model the expected task outcomes for them. The topic or content behind the presentation may also see students being able to establish a more personal connection with you, especially if the topic is one that involves their interests such as hobbies and family.

Step one – Identify

Identify the type of assignment or work that you will have your students turn into a presentation. Also, identify if the topic is best suited for in-class work or homework, and for students to work on individually, in pairs, or as a group. Further, depending on the teaching context and the age of students, it might be advisable to have each student initially present solo or on a topic that they are familiar with (for example, themselves, a place, or a favorite thing), then later work collaboratively on a presentation surrounding an unfamiliar topic that would require research (for example, explaining vocabulary or idioms, providing a tutorial, or giving a demonstration).

Step two – Familiarize

Provide examples, and ensure that students are familiar with how to design a Prezi, and how to use the software to create a multimedia-based presentation. To this end, develop a Prezi of your own following a similar topic that you will want students to provide a presentation on. Then, work with students to explain how to use the software while building a template or outline that students can then later use as a model to follow when beginning work on their own presentations or when working with peers.

Step three – Develop

Ensure that each student has access to the completed outline that was built as part of the Prezi tutorial. This is worthwhile as it ensures that all students have the same template to work from, and provides a framework to begin to integrate content in order to build a final presentation for delivery. It will also be less time-consuming for students to develop a presentation from an outline, so focus can be placed more on actual language use as well as the development of multimedia-based items for inclusion in the project. It also provides students with a precise format to follow (so it is teacher-guided), and with motivation to include or develop the appropriate content (so it is student-centered).

Step four – Present

The Prezi presentation paradigm allows for both on and offline presentation as well as submission as homework or for delivery as an in-class presentation. Each of these presentation options will depend on the specific teaching and learning context as well as the topic, but if delivered as an in-class presentation, then it will help build learner confidence as students start to use the language that they have learned in front of others while sharing their own ideas and thoughts (be they professional or personal ones). This in turn can also make the language learning process more personal and more interesting.

Step five – Grade and give feedback

Providing appropriate and timely feedback is also important. You should be prepared to use an evaluation rubric, such as one that can be found in this book, and to give feedback not only on the presentation itself but also on the students' English language abilities (pronunciation, grammar, vocabulary), body language (gestures, stance), and voice projection. Also consider whether this feedback should be given publicly or privately.

Step six – Distribute

If desired, the Prezi can be shared on social media, or embedded within a class blog post or a page on a learning management system (LMS) such as Moodle. Each presentation would then be available for all students to review as required, and for other stakeholders (such as parents and administration) to view at leisure.

14
Photocopiable material

This section of the book contains photocopiable handouts, and you can feel free to make as many copies as you require for teaching purposes and for use within your classes. Any other use or distribution should include a citation to the source of the content.

Providing students with a handout to use during development of any presentation, multimedia or otherwise, can help guide them in the development of their project, as well as the media resources that they may ultimately wish to select to accompany it. An example has been provided here. This also allows students to work on their presentation project without being tied to the use of technology. Also provided is a lesson plan template that can be used for considering how best to integrate the steps for using the Prezi presentation paradigm with classes. As such, the template is meant to act as means to begin thinking about how to implement, with your classes, aspects of what has been discovered through this book. The template should be supplemented with any necessary material, along with the staging as well as other aspects of the lesson being adjusted as required.

The following photocopiable material is available:
- Prezi presentation preparation resource notes
- Prezi presentation preparation handout
- Prezi practice exercise and tutorial
- Prezi presentation tips
- Lesson plan template

Prezi Presentation Preparation
Resource Notes

Prezi Title	Group Members
A title is chosen by students, and written here.	Student names are listed here.

Description

Students will answer one or all of the following questions here:

1. What are you trying to communicate?
2. What content will help support your message?
3. What structure or view path will your presentation contain, and in how many frames/slides?
4. What hook or imagery will you use to capture the audience at the start of the Prezi?

Media Resources

Students list all of the media that they will need for their presentation. This will help them later to search for the right material. They will need to consider:

1. Music, songs, voice recordings
2. Photo/video, images, diagrams, documents PowerPoints
3. Text, titles, animation effects

Prezi Canvas

Students can use this space to begin sketching a layout of the frames and the view path of their presentation.

Prezi Presentation Preparation Handout

Prezi Title	Group Members

Description

Media Resources

Prezi Canvas

Prezi Practice Exercise and Tutorial

Step One – Make your Prezi

To start out:

- Select the 'My Prezis' Tab.
- Then, click 'Create a new Prezi'.

Step Two – Select a theme

Search for a template or make a selection from those presented, then click 'Use template', or click 'Start blank Prezi'. For example, search for a theme like 'sport'. For this exercise:

- Click 'Start a blank Prezi'.

Step Three – The Prezi canvas

The top menu

Use the menu across the top of the screen to add a title, undo, redo, save, insert various media elements, customize aspects of the background or themes, to start presenting, share the Prezi, change the settings, or to exit the Prezi. For this exercise:

- Click in the title section, and type the text 'Sports'.

Left side menu

Use the side menu on the left to add new frames, or change the type of frame to be added to the presentation canvas. There should be one frame on the Prezi presentation canvas already. So, for this example, add two more frames. These two additional frames can be any of the options available (e.g. bracket, circle, rectangle, or invisible). For this exercise:

- Select 'Circle'.
- Then, hover the mouse over the frame with a plus icon, click on it and drag the new frame to the Prezi canvas.
- Place the frame by letting go of the mouse. The frame can be moved around, and placed by clicking on it and using the hand icon.
- The plus and minus buttons, or the transform icons can be used for resizing.

Right side menu

The side menu to the right can be used for various functions, including changing the zoom level or to show an overview of the entire presentation canvas. For this exercise:

- Click on the 'Plus' icon to zoom in.
- Then click on the 'Minus' icon to zoom out. Keep in mind that the mouse can also be used to zoom in and out.
- Finally, click on the 'House' icon to return to a zoom level that will show an overview of the entire Prezi.

Step Four – Inserting Text

To add text to the Prezi presentation canvas, click anywhere within the Prezi window, and begin typing. Text can be set as a title, subtitle, or body, and various font elements can be chosen such as font size and type, bulleting, and justification. For this exercise:

- Click near the top of the Prezi above the first frame, and type the word 'Sports'.
- Set the text as a title, and then place it appropriately.
- The text frame can be moved by clicking the hand icon, and resized using the plus and minus icons or by dragging the transform icons around the edge of the frame.
- The style of the frame can then be added as a favorite.

Step Five – Working with Content

Adding Content

From the top menu, select 'Insert'. A number of various types of content can then be inserted, including images from a file, symbols and shapes from a searchable index, YouTube videos, favorite items, a single frame or multi-frame layout, arrows, lines, highlights, background music from a file, a PDF, and a video or a PowerPoint from a file. For this exercise:

- Select 'Symbols & shapes', then in the search box type a search term or select an image like the bicycle.

- To select the bicycle image, click on it, then drag it to the Prezi canvas. The image can then be moved around by clicking the hand icon, and resized using the plus and minus icons or by dragging the transform icons around the edge of the frame surrounding the image.

- Options along the top of the image frame allow you to 'Crop' the image, 'favorite' the image, 'delete' the image, or 'replace' it.

Step Six – Working with Frames

Frame menu options

When a frame is selected, several menu options are available, including 'Zoom to frame', changing the 'Type' of frame, changing the color of the frame, adding the frame as a 'Favorite' or 'Delete'.

Grouping and Resizing with a frame

For this exercise:

- Move the image that you previously placed on the Prezi canvas to fit inside this new frame.
- After that, move the frame to any position that you like. You will notice that anything inside a frame will move with the frame.
- Click the frame to select it, and from the menu options, use the plus or minus buttons to change the size. You will notice that any content within the frame will also resize proportionally.

Adding animation to frames

To add animations to the content of a frame, right click on the frame, then select 'Animate frame contents'. For this exercise:

- 'Right click' on the frame with the image of the bicycle.
- Then, in the editing window, select the image and click on 'Add a fade in' effect.
- You can then preview the animation or click on 'Done' to return to the presentation canvas.

Step Seven – Editing the Viewing Path

Frame order

As you have been preparing your Prezi, you may have noticed that each frame has a number to the side of it. If the presentation is played as a slideshow, this number indicates when that particular frame will be shown. For this exercise:

- Click on the 'House' icon to see the entire presentation canvas. Note the numbers next to each frame showing their view order.

Changing frame order

When editing the frame viewing order, you will see that all the frame numbers are connected by a line to show the viewing path, and objects can be added between frames by dragging the plus icon of any of these lines to those objects. For this exercise:

- Click 'Edit path' found on the left side menu at the bottom to start work on changing the viewing order.

Setting the viewing order

The viewing order will be displayed on the left side menu by slide, and these slides can also be reordered. For this exercise:

- Click 'Clear all', under 'Edit path', and then click on the title text. This will then be labeled '1' and moved to the first slide position on the left menu.
- Next, click on each frame in the order that you would like to set them for presentation. The frames should now be labeled '2', '3', '4' respectively and added to the left slide menu. If desired, reorder the slides.
- Click 'Done' from the top menu.

Step Eight – Showing and Reviewing the Prezi

It is always a good idea to review your Prezi before it is exported or shared with a wider audience, and to make any necessary edits or adjustments as necessary. For this exercise:

- From the top menu, click 'Present'. This will then play the presentation in full screen mode, and you can move through the steps of the viewing path using the right or left arrows.
- Pressing 'esc' will exit the presentation mode and return you to editing.
- You can now work on improving the presentation.

Step Nine – Exporting and Sharing the Prezi

Once you have played back your Prezi, and are happy with the final review, you may choose to export it or to share it.

To export the Prezi

Click the 'Share' icon on the top menu, and select one of the following options:

- Click 'Download as PDF' to save the Prezi as a PDF file, with each frame or slide becoming a page.
- Click 'Download as portable Prezi' to obtain a zip file containing the presentation.

To share the Prezi

Click the 'Share' icon on the top menu, and select one of the options below:

- Click 'Share Prezi' to obtain a link to the Prezi, and be able to add people (by email address) who can view the Prezi. Options to set the privacy and duplication settings for the Prezi are also available here.
- Click 'Present remotely' to obtain a link that allows a maximum of thirty invited people to watch a remote presentation of the Prezi at the same time as you navigate and present.
- Click 'Share on Facebook' to obtain a link to email as well as the ability to share the Prezi on social media.

Prezi Presentation Tips

1. Start by mind mapping your presentation.
2. Use templates to help you get started.
3. Use 'Redo' or 'Undo' when editing.
4. Use magnifier buttons '+' or '-' to zoom in and out while you edit and present.
5. Use the highlighter to point out key information.
6. Zoom in on objects to give them focus.
7. Use the zoom tool sparingly.
8. Credit the sources that you use in your Prezi, including research and image-based resources.
9. Keep in mind that although Prezi auto-saves, you still need to click 'Save' and 'Exit' when you finish editing.
10. Stand to the left when presenting, as this will give your audience an anchor when reading the screen.

Lesson Plan Template	
Teaching Context	
Level of Proficiency and Maturity	
Lesson Length	
Lesson Topic	
Objectives	
Outcomes	
Relevant Prior Learning	
Teacher Preparation	
Hardware	
Software	
Webpage Links	
Additional Resources	

Procedure			
Stage and Timing	Objective	Teacher	Students
Review Stage (if required)			
Warm-up Stage/Pre-Technology Use			
Main Stage/ Technology-based Activity			
Practice Stage			
Lesson Summation Stage/Post-Technology Activities			

Further Considerations	
Follow-Up Activities	
Contingency Plan(s)	
Evaluation	

15

Resources list

As sites continuously go down, merge, and emerge, perhaps only a small selection of all appropriate resource content should be presented here. An attempt at keeping the number of resources to a select few for each type also provides a sample that is both comprehensive and extensive, but not overwhelming. Like any other instructor resource list, individuals will be able to add to the content as they find material that is useful, creating their own bookmark list, and over time, come to curate a vast resource library tailored to their individual teaching and learning context. Each section of this list is broken down into applications that are mostly all freely available for use with Android or iOS devices, computers, or web-based platforms.

Teachers who wish to make notes, or to record any additional resources that they come across, can use the notes section at the end of this chapter.

The following content is covered:

- App creation
- Audio creation/editing
- Blogs
- Bookmarking
- Books
- Coding
- Comic strip generators
- Copyright
- Digital story creation
- Image resources
- Image editing
- Interactive whiteboards
- Mashups
- Media timelines
- Music resources
- Podcasting
- Podcatchers
- Presentations
- Publishing
- QR codes
- Rubrics
- Screencasting
- Storyboarding and scripting
- Story creation apps
- Video editing
- Video resources
- WebQuests
- Wikis

App Creation

Android – n/a

iOS – n/a

Computer – n/a

Web

Android Creator [free/paid] creates free Android apps without the need for programming knowledge.

AppMakr [free/paid] is a template based application creator that relies on drag and drop of elements for the development of no-coding required applications. It is available in a variety of languages.

Appy Pie [free/paid] relies on templates as well as drag and drop for users to begin creating their app. It requires no coding skills.

AppYourself [paid] is an app creation tool aimed at the business market.

Como DIY [paid] is a do-it-yourself app creation tool aimed to mostly target to businesses, and is available in a number of languages.

iBuildApp [paid] is a template driven app creator for iPhone and Android phones.

Audio Creation/Editing

Android

   PCM Recorder [free] is a simple voice recorder.

   Pocket WavePad [free] records edits and adds effects to audio.

   TapeMachine [paid] is a graphical sound recorder and editor.

iOS

   Pocket WavePad [free] records edits and adds effects to audio.

   Voice Memos [paid] is voice recorder that allows multitasking.

Computer

   Audacity [free] is an open source digital editing program available for Mac and PC which you can use to record, edit and mix narration and music.

   Pocket WavePad [free] records, edits, and adds effects to audio for Mac.

GoldWave [free/paid] is a digital audio editor that provides simple recording as well as more sophisticated processing, restoration, enhancement, and conversion for Windows and Linux. A free version is available for evaluation purposes, after which a lifetime license can be purchased.

Web

Twistedwave [free] is a browser-based audio editor that can record or edit any audio file.

Blogs

Android

Blogaway [free] is a simple application to allow blogging on-the-go. It works with Blogger and allows for post creation, adding of photos, videos, multiple account management, saving of drafts, bookmarking, and a host of formatting options.

iOS

Disqus [free] is a commenting system that can be included in blogs as an add-on. The application provides an easy way to moderate comments and publish responses to keep engagement levels high.

TravelPod – Travel Blog [free] is a blogging application that works on- and offline, and is designed to be used while traveling.

Computer – n/a

Web

Blogger.com [free] will host your blog for free, and aside from being very easy to use, it allows some level of privacy so it can be suitable for use as a class blogging site. From a single account, you can create as many blogs as you wish and determine who is allowed to comment on the content.

BuzzSumo [paid] allows users to search for blog posts that have been highly shared across social media.

Edublogs.org [free] allows teachers to create and mange their own and students' websites. There is room for customization of design and the ability to add various media to this private and secure platform.

Kidblog.org [free] is an easy-to-use, safe, and secure publishing platform designed for students in grades K-12. There are a number of excellent features including privacy and password protection, and there is no need for student personal information to be collected, nor is there any advertising. It is free for up to fifty students per class.

WordPress.org [free] is one of the most popular blogging platforms in use today as it is open-source and is easily customizable. The downloadable software for self-hosting purposes is much more flexible than that available on the blogging platform.

Twitter [free] deserves a mention here as it is useful for microblogging (posting short frequent updates). It allows users to post and read short 140-character posts called 'tweets'.

Tumblr [free] is a blogging platform open to those over thirteen years of age, with most users using pen names over their real names when blogging. Users can post on their blog, follow others, and search posts. It is unique in that posts are divided into media types: text, photo, quote, link, chat, audio, and video.

Bookmarking

Android

Bookmark [free] is a cross-platform app that allows for the syncing of bookmarks across different browsers and devices.

Delicious [free] provides users with the ability to organize links to content on the internet that they would like to save, the ability to discover links, edit tags and comments, and also to explore content saved by friends.

Facebook Save [free] is a built-in option for saving Facebook news content to read at a later date.

Instapaper [free] provides an offline archiving solution for web pages, and it presents this content to be read in newspaper fashion. Content can be highlighted, and notes can be added while reading.

Pinterest [free] allows users to pin posts (for example, web pages, images, and videos) and organize them around a common theme.

Pocket [free] integrates with a large number of third party applications that allow for the building of bookmarks. Web pages, videos, images, and whatever else can be used offline for bookmarking. Archiving maintains the links but removes the content from offline availability.

iOS

Delicious [free] allows users to save content from the internet (including web pages, blog posts, tweets, pictures, and video), and provides options for searching through others' collections of links.

Facebook Save [free] is a built-in option for saving Facebook news content to read at a later date.

Instapaper [free] provides an offline archiving solution for web pages and presents this content to be read in newspaper fashion. Content can be highlighted, and notes can be added while reading.

Pinterest [free] allows users to pin posts (for example, web pages, images, and videos) and organize them around a common theme.

Pocket [free] integrates with a large number of third party applications that allow for the building of bookmarks. Web pages, videos, images, and whatever else can be used offline for bookmarking. Archiving maintains the links but removes the content from offline availability.

Computer

EdwinSoft's UltimateDemon [paid] is link building software that helps to provide search engine optimization to a website.

Pinterest [free] allows users to pin posts (for example, web pages, images, and videos) and organize them around a common theme.

Pocket [free] integrates with a large number of third party applications that allow for the building of bookmarks. Web pages, videos, images, and whatever else can be used offline for bookmarking. Archiving maintains the links but removes the content from offline availability.

ReadKit [trial/paid] offers an Apple Mac curative and archiving platform for the content found in your other bookmarking applications (like Pocket and Instapaper) and RSS readers, and provides an extra level of organization to this content.

Web

Delicious [free] is a social bookmarking site that allows users to bookmark webpages to the internet instead of locally.

Facebook Save [free] is a built-in option for saving Facebook news content to read at a later date.

Instapaper [free] provides an offline archiving solution for web pages, and it presents this content to be read in newspaper fashion. Content can be highlighted, and notes can be added while reading.

OnlyWire [paid] works with WordPress and offers automatic submission of content to social networking and social bookmarking sites.

Pocket [free] integrates with a large number of third party applications that allow for the building of bookmarks. Web pages, videos, images, and whatever else can be used offline for bookmarking. Archiving maintains the links but removes the content from offline availability.

Books

Android

Wattpad Free Books [free] provides access to free stories and books written by aspiring authors.

iOS

Free Books – Ultimate Classics Library [free] features free access to 23,469 classic books.

Computer – n/a

Web

BookRix [free] allows access to thousands of books to read either online or to download as ebooks.

Children's Storybooks Online [free] provides a series of illustrated stories for all ages to read.

Coding

Android

Run Marco! [free] offers users the opportunity to play an adventure game while they learn to code. The application presents instructions using 'Blocky', which is the same as that used by the official Hour of Code tutorials.

Tynker [free] is an easy way for children to learn programming skills as they solve puzzles to learn concepts and build games, or control robots and drones. A number of templates are available for free.

iOS

Codea [paid] is a software development tool that uses the Lua programming language to teach users how to program.

Hopscotch [free] is an application that allows users to begin learning to code by making games similar to Angry Birds, and sharing them so others can play them.

ScratchJr [free] allows users to program their own interactive stories and games by snapping together graphical programming blocks. The application was inspired by the Scratch programming language.

Tynker [free] is an easy way for children to learn programming skills as they solve puzzles to learn concepts and build games, or control robots and drones. A number of templates are available for free.

Computer

Scratch [free] allows users to create stories, games, and animations using the Scratch programming language, and then share these with others. It is a project of the Lifelong Kindergarten Group at the MIT Media Lab.

Lightbot – Programming Puzzles [paid] is an OS X game-based application that allows players to use programming logic to solve levels. The app is also available for Android and iOS devices.

Web – n/a

Comic Strip Generators

Android

Comic Maker [free] creates comics from the photo gallery.

Comic Strip It! Lite [free] takes photos or use photo gallery images to create a comic.

iOS

Comic Life 3 [paid] turns photos into comic pages, or creates an entire comic from scratch using templates to build pages with speech balloons, comic lettering, and photo filters.

ToonTastic [free] is a wizard-based animated comic or cartoon creator.

Strip Designer [paid] is software for comic creation that uses camera, library, or Facebook photo options to create a comic.

Computer

Comic Creator [paid] is a basic template driven comic creator for use on a Windows computer.

Web

Pixton [free/paid] is an easy to use comprehensive online comic creator that supports narration, and offers a range of signup options from a free fun option to paid educator/business accounts.

MakeBeliefsComix [free] is a basic comic creator that uses black and white images over a four-panel comic strip. An iOS version is also available.

Toonlet [free] allows for anyone to create their own cartoon characters and web comics.

Toondoo [free] allows for the drag and drop creation of comic strips. An iOS version is also available.

Copyright

Android – n/a

iOS – n/a

Computer – n/a

Web

> *Creative Commons Licenses* [free] gives detailed information regarding the various types of licensing afforded to creative commons, and the permissions that each license grants for the use specific works.

> *Image Codr* [free] can assist learners and teachers alike in determining how a Flickr image can be used (as determined by the original photographer), and provides users with an automatically generated Creative Commons citation regarding the images use within digital projects.

Digital Story Creation

Android

Com-Phone Story Maker [free] combines audio, photos, and text to create stories while allowing for three different layers of audio.

WeVideo [free] is a web-based video editor that can mix images, text, video, and audio.

iOS

30hands [free] creates a story by adding narration to photos.

Magisto [free] uses a wizard to create a short video based on provided images or video content.

Splice [free/paid] combines photos, videos, music and narrations. Effects and transitions can be added.

WeVideo [free] is a web-based video editor that can mix images, text, video, and audio.

Computer

iMovie [paid] provides video creation and editing software that can create easily shareable content on a Mac. An iOS version is available.

Microsoft Photo Story 3 [free] for Windows lets you create slideshows from a wizard that includes audio, narration, and images.

Windows Movie Maker [free] for Windows operating systems is a video editing software application that allows for narration, audio, images, and video to be mixed and edited, and it comes with transitions and special effects.

Web

Animoto [paid] allows users to submit songs, choose a theme, add their photos, videos, and text to create a digital story that they can share.

Meograph [free] is a digital storytelling tool that relies on Google Earth to create map-based and timeline-based narrated stories.

WeVideo [free] is a web-based video editor that can mix images, text, video, and audio.

Image Resources

Android – n/a

iOS – n/a

Computer – n/a

Web

Cagle Cartoons [free] provides access to a number of political cartoons from around the world. The images are organized by topic with artists categorized by country.

Flickr Creative Commons [free] provides images that can be used for almost any educational project, as long as proper citation is followed

FreeFoto.com [free] has a photos area that is available under three licensing options: recognition, Creative Commons, and commercial.

Morguefile [free] provides a range of images that are copyright free, and are available for use with few or no restrictions.

Pics4Learning.com [free] is a website that provides safe and free images for educational uses. Images here are copyright-friendly and can be used for classrooms, multimedia projects, websites, videos, portfolios, or other projects.

PicSearch [free] allows you to search the internet for images, but be aware that the image may not be copyright-free, or that it may require permission to be used in projects or in any other educational contexts.

The Library of Congress Prints & Photographs Online Catalog [free] makes an attempt to ensure that as many of their images as possible are available online in a digital format.

Wikimedia [free] serves as a point from where all the images and video posted in Wikipedia can be viewed. Most of the images found here are either copyright-free or free for use with minimal restrictions.

Image Editing
Android
PicSay [free] can edit photos, overlay titles, and add special effects.

FX Camera [free] is a photo booth app that allows users to add various effects to photographs.

iOS
PhotoPad [free] can create, edit, and save vector illustrations. It can also work with photo library images.

ScreenChomp [free] allows you to share, explain, and markup images.

Computer
PhotoPad [paid] is an image editor for OS X.

PaintShop Pro [paid] is a comprehensive image editing package for Windows.

Web
Adobe Photoshop CC [paid] is a comprehensive cloud-based image editing package.

Phixr [free] is an online photo editor with various filters and effects, and it can connect to various social media sites.

FotoFlexer [free] is an online image editor offering a number of effects, distortions, and other features.

Pixlr [paid] is a comprehensive online photo editing app.

Interactive Whiteboards

Android

ExplainEverything [free] allows users to share their content by using an interactive screencasting whiteboard.

Interactive Whiteboard [free] is a virtual whiteboard that can be used for drawing or teaching various concepts as it allows for multiple finger input, straight line drawing mode, drawing move mode, and various other features.

PPT and Whiteboard Sharing [free] provides a way to share presentations, videos, and drawings in various settings including the classroom, the boardroom, and online meetings.

Whiteboard: Collaborative Draw [free] is a collaborative drawing application that allows real-time painting.

iOS

Doceri [trial/paid] combines screencasting, desktop control, and an interactive whiteboard in one application, with control through Airplay or through Mac or PC.

Educreations Interactive Whiteboard [free] is an interactive whiteboard and screencasting tool that allows annotation, animation, and narration of a number of content types.

Screenchomp [free] allows users to annotate pictures or to use the application as a whiteboard. Any work completed with the application can be saved automatically to the internet.

ShowMe Interactive Whiteboard [free] allows voice-over recording of whiteboard interactions so that tutorials can be created easily before being shared online.

Computer

Open Sakore [free] is open-source and it is dedicated to teacher and student use. It allows for insertion of multiple document types, along with annotation capabilities for commenting drawing and highlighting content.

Smoothboard Air [free] is a collaborative interactive whiteboard for multiple iPads and for Android tablets. It allows users to annotate desktop applications wirelessly through the use of a web browser.

Web

A Web Whiteboard [free] is a online whiteboard application that allows a number of devices (like computers, tablets, and smartphones), to draw sketches, and to collaborate with others around the globe.

Realtime Board [free] is a whiteboard in a browser that allows for collaboration among a number of users.

Twiddla [free] is a web-based meeting environment that allows users to mark up photos, graphics, and websites, or to just start out with a blank canvas.

Web Whiteboard [free] is a simple way to draw and write together online by creating an online whiteboard with a click, and sharing it live or by sending the link to others.

Mashups

Android

Edjing 5 DJ Music Mixer [free] not only transforms any android device into a turntable, but it provides access to a range of music libraries.

iOS

iMashup [paid] is a professional quality remixing app that allows users to create their own mashups and remixes.

Pacemaker [free] allows users to create and save mixes on an iPhone or iWatch, and to DJ live from iPad devices.

Computer

Mixxx [free] is an advanced open source DJ package that includes an extensive array of features for OS X and Windows.

Web

Mashstix [free] is a website with user submitted mashups available.

Media Timelines

Android

RWT Timelines [free] allows students to create a graphical representation of any event or process by displaying items sequentially along a line. The final product can be exported as a pdf, or saved to the device's camera roll.

Timeline [free] allows users to create timelines and associate them with colors, and to view multiple timelines together. It is a useful reference tool for remembering dates.

iOS

TimelineBuilder [paid] allows users to create custom timelines with images and text with unique beginning and end dates.

Timeline Maker [free] provides an easy way to display a series of events in a chronological order.

Computer

Edraw Timeline Maker [paid] is a tool that makes it simple to create a professional looking timeline, history, schedule, time table, or project plan diagram from scratch.

TimelineMaker [paid] provides a simplified timeline charting tool aimed at project planners, and business professionals, and those in educational contexts.

Web

Capzles [free] allows users to create rich multimedia experiences from videos, photos, music, blogs, and documents by integrating these into a timeline of sequential events, and then share them on various social media platforms.

Hstry [free] is specifically designed for the education sector, and it allows teachers and students to create interactive timelines for assignments and online sharing.

OurStory [free] offers a means for creating story-based timelines with pictures.

Timeline [free] from *readwritethink* allows students of all ages to easily create a graphical representation of related items or events in sequential order and display them along a line using various images and text.

TimeGlider [free] is a web-based timeline project creator that allows zooming and panning across timelines. Users are able to set the size of events as they relate to importance.

Tiki-Toki [free/paid] is a web-based timeline editor that allows viewing of timelines in 3D, and it allows for the integration of images and videos.

WhenInTime [free] is a web application for creating and sharing media-based timelines.

Music Resources

Android

FindSounds [free] can be used to search the internet for sounds that can then be saved as ringtones, notifications, or alarms.

Shazam [free] allows Android device users to identify the music playing around them, as well as discover song lyrics, and other music related information and tracks.

iOS

Shazam [free] allows iOS device users to identify the music playing around them, as well as discover song lyrics, and other music related information and tracks.

Computer – n/a

Web

300 Monks [free] provides a comprehensive source of royalty free music.

ccMixter [free] is a free music site that is community based and promotes a remix culture. *A cappella* and remix tracks licensed under Creative Commons are available for download and use in creative works.

FMA (Free Music Archive) [free] provides access to a range of free music based on a wide variety of genre. The music is offered free under various licenses for use.

Find Sounds [free] is a long-running service that can be used to search the internet for various sounds that can then be incorporated into various projects.

FreePlay Music [free] is a service that searches the internet for free music that can be used in YouTube videos and other projects.

Podcasting

Android

Podomatic Podcast & Mix Player [free] provides access to a wide variety of podcasts, listening in offline mode, and features such as a dynamic social feed so you can see the podcasts Facebook friends follow and like.

iOS

PodOmatic Podcast Player [free] provides access to a wide variety of podcasts, listening in offline mode, and features such as a dynamic social feed so you can see the podcasts Facebook friends follow and like.

Computer

Audacity [free] is a free multi-track audio recorder and editor with some very powerful features that include those for adding effects to files and conducting analysis of the audio recorded.

iTunes [free] offers media on demand and a way to organize and enjoy music, movies, and TV shows, as well as accessing and subscribing to podcasts and screencasts.

LoudBlog [free] is a Content Management System (CMS) for podcasts. This program automatically generates skinnable websites and RSS-feeds for audio and video podcasts, including provision for show notes and links.

PodcastGenerator [free] is an open source content management system for podcast publishing. It provides a comprehensive range of tools to manage all aspects of podcast publishing.

PodProducer [free] allows for the recording of voice and the adding of effects.

Web

ESLPod [free] provides a range of podcast content tailored to second-language learners of English from specific topics through to test-taking guides.

FeedForAll [free] allows for the creation, editing, and publishing of RSS feeds.

Feedity [free] is an online tool for creating an RSS feed for any web page, with an option to upgrade to a premium account that offers additional features.

FETCHRSS: RSS Generator [free] is an online RSS feed generator, that can create a feed out of almost any web page, automatically updates the RSS feed when new content is added to the web page, and generates an RSS for a social networking site.

OPML Viewer [free] allows users to view the contents of outline processor markup language (OPML) files.

Podcast Alley [free] is the place to go if you are interested in podcasts, want to gain access to the top podcasts, and want to find out the latest news about podcasts.

Pod Gallery [free] is a podcasting website where podcasters can share their episodes, and where listeners can subscribe.

QT-ESL Podcasts [free] provides a range of podcasts that cover oral grammar practice and includes scripts and worksheets.

SoundCloud [free] is a social sound platform where anyone is able to create and share audio.

Podcatchers

Android

Podcast Player [free] provides a range of podcast discovery options and tools, along with a range of features including a sleep timer, video support, intelligent silence skip and volume boost, as well as support for tablet, Chromecast, and Android Wear.

Podcast Republic [free] is an application that is ad-supported. It offers a variety of features from podcast discovery and automatic downloading through to storage management, sleep timer, and car mode. Support is also included from Chromecast and Android Wear.

Pocket Casts [paid] shows subscribed podcasts in a tile format, with easy sorting and categorization functions. Video podcast is also supported, along with auto-download and cleanup of downloaded and played episodes to save on storage space. Several features allow it to stand out, including a sleep timer as well as its cross-platform nature that grants it the ability to sync between multiple devices and mobile operating systems.

iOS

Overcast: Podcast Player [free] provides a combination of powerful audio and podcast management features. The application comes with a wide variety of features that allow it to download episodes, send notifications of new episodes, and play content offline or by streaming. It can also normalize speech levels, and speed through gaps and silence in podcasts.

Castro: High Fidelty Podcasts [free] is a simple and easy to use podcatcher. It provides a simple design with automatic episode download, dynamic storage management, along with episode streaming.

Pocket Casts [paid] shows subscribed podcasts in a tile format, with easy sorting and categorization functions. Video podcast is also supported, along with auto-download and cleanup of downloaded and played episodes to save on storage space. Several features allow it to stand out, including a sleep timer as well as its cross-platform nature that grants it the ability to sync between multiple devices and mobile operating systems.

Computer

gPodder [free] is an open source media aggregator and podcast client. It is able to store information in the cloud on which shows you have listened to, and it allows for the local installation of the client for download of content.

iTunes [free] is a comprehensive media aggregator that provides comprehensive support for media management, the audio and video playback of local media, podcast search and subscription, along with automatic downloads, syncing and streaming, and many other features.

Juice [free] is a long-standing cross platform no-frills podcast aggregator that is open source, and specifically designed to manage podcasts. Features include auto cleanup, centralized feed management, and for Windows users, accessibility options for the blind and visually impaired.

Web

Cloud Caster [free] is a web-based podcaster which works across all mobile devices. It syncs progress and playlists across platforms, and provides search and support for audio and video podcasts.

Presentations

Android

Glogster [free] allows students using an Android-based device to create online multimedia posters, or Glogs, from a combination of media types (from audio, graphic, to video), and hyperlinks.

Google Slides [free] allows Android device users with a Google account a means of creating, editing, and collaborating with others on presentations.

LinkedIn SlideShare [free] allows Android device users the ability to search and explore for a variety of presentations, infographics, and documents on topics of their interest.

Microsoft PowerPoint [free] allows users to view PowerPoint presentations on their device for free, and to make edits and changes on the go.

iOS

Glogster [free] allows students using an iOS device to create online multimedia posters, or Glogs, from a combination of media types (from audio, graphic, to video), and hyperlinks.

Google Slides [free] allows iOS device users with a Google account a means of creating, editing, and collaborating with others on presentations.

Keynote [free] is a powerful presentation app that allows users to develop comprehensive presentations with animations, transitions, and multimedia elements.

LinkedIn SlideShare [free] allows iOS device users the ability to search and explore for a variety of presentations, infographics, and documents on topics of their interest.

Microsoft PowerPoint [free] allows users to view PowerPoint presentations on their device for free, and to make edits and changes on the go.

Computer

Microsoft PowerPoint [paid] is a comprehensive presentation software application, and is perhaps the most used and recognizable.

Keynote [free] is a powerful presentation app that allows users to develop comprehensive presentations with animations, transitions, and multimedia elements.

Web

Bunkr [free] is a presentation tool that displays any online content including social media posts, images, videos, audio, articles, and files.

Glogster [free] allows students to create online multimedia posters, or Glogs, from a combination of media types (from audio, graphic, to video), and hyperlinks.

Google Slides [free] allows those with a Google account, a means of creating, editing, and collaborating with others on presentations.

LinkedIn SlideShare [free] allows users to search for presentations, infographics, documents and other items on topics of their interest.

Microsoft PowerPoint Online [free] extends the Microsoft PowerPoint experience to the web browser with OneDrive integration, and allows users to create, edit, and view files on the go.

Prezi [free] is a visually oriented presentation packaged that also allows users to upload PowerPoint slides, and customize them, or use a variety of their own images, text, audio, and video.

Slidebean [free] offers a one-click presentation development system that incorporates a variety of templates into the design of presentations.

Slides [free] is a place for creating, presenting, and sharing slide decks.

Swipe [free] allows users to share a presentation link with anyone across any device, and it allows viewers to interact with the presentation on several levels, from collaboration through to taking polls.

VoiceThread [free] allows users to import various media such as images, PowerPoints, and PDFs. It provides a means of making audio or video recordings concerning those media artifacts, and it also allows other users to reply to the initial comments, by audio or video means, as the presentation progresses.

Publishing

Android

Book Creator Free [free] offers a simple means of creating a variety of ebooks including picture books, comic and photo books, and journals and textbooks. It allows for the use of images, narration, texts, annotations and drawings.

Book Writer Free [free] is a simple book creation application that allows users to share their content with others.

My Story Builder [free] is a simple, 'suitable for children', book editor.

Scribble: Kids Book Maker [paid] is an application that allows children to write, illustrate, and publish their own comprehensive stories in a range of formations including video export. It contains a series of story starters, stickers, and backgrounds to help them work on creating stories from the start.

iOS

Book Creator Free [free] offers a simple means of creating a variety of ebooks including picture books, comic and photo books, and journals and textbooks. It allows for the use of images, narration, texts, annotations and drawings.

Creative Book Builder [paid] is a professional ebook editor and generator which can also extend the utility of ebooks through the use of a range of widgets.

Demibooks Composer Pro [free] builds interactive books with animation, audio, images, and effects.

Scribble Press – Creative Book Maker for Kids [paid] contains a series of story starters, stickers and backgrounds to help get young kids working on creating stories that can be turned into ebooks.

Computer

Android Book App Maker [paid] provides users with the ability to turn content into a flip-book app.

iBooks Author [free] provides a series of templates and styles to assist in the development of ebooks for the iBook store.

Kotobee [free] provides free software to assist in the creation of ebooks and libraries for a range of platforms.

Web

Blurb [paid] is just one of many online services that can assist in the creation of ebooks.

QR Codes

Android

I-nigma QR & Barcode Scanner (free) is a versatile barcode and QR code reader that can scan a multitude of codes and share these codes as well.

QR Code Reader (free) is a simple QR Code and product barcode scanner.

QR Droid Code Scanner (free) is a powerful barcode, QR code, and Data Matrix scanner that offers multi-language support.

iOS

Bakodo – Barcode Scanner and QR Barcode Reader (free) scans all types of QR codes and barcodes.

QR Reader for iPhone (free) scans a variety of codes including QR codes and barcodes, and features auto-detect scanning.

QRafter – QR Code and Barcode Reader and Generator (free) is a two-dimensional barcode scanner for iOS. Along with a variety of useful features, it can scan and generate QR codes.

Computer

CodeTwo QR Code Desktop Reader (free) allows users to scan QR codes directly from their screen onto their desktop. Users select the QR code to be read by selecting the area with a QR code using their mouse.

QR-Code Studio (free) is for Mac and Windows computers. The QR code maker software is freeware.

Web

QR Code Generator (free) creates QR codes, in a limited number of formats, for free.

QR Stuff QR Code Generator (free) creates QR codes from a various types of data such as website URLs, image files, PDF files, and so on, with static and dynamic embedding options.

The QR Code Generator (free) allows for the free scan and generation of QR codes for a variety of uses.

Rubrics

Android

Daily Rubric: Any Curriculum [free] allows teachers to create and use rubrics from their Android device. Rubrics can be designed from curriculum outcomes, or based on the pre-loaded Common Core Standards.

iOS

Easy Assessment [paid] offers a means to capture and assess performance based on custom created rubrics, scale, or criteria.

Rubrics [paid] allows instructors to track student performance and produce reports based on custom rubrics and grading options.

Computer – n/a

Web

Kathy Shrock's Guide to Everything: Assessment and Rubrics [free] provides access to a wide range of rubrics to help guide assessment of students.

iRubric [free] is a website where instructors can create their own rubrics, or they can build off those made available from other instructors.

RubiStar [free] allows instructors to create their own rubrics using templates designed for core subjects as well as art, music, and multimedia.

Screencasting

Android

AZ Screen Recorder [free] is a screen recording application that offers several features, including the ability to capture the front camera as well as screen recording. It also provides video trimming.

ilos Screen Recorder [free] is a simple application that records the screen and provides audio capture as well.

Telecine [free] is an open source application that allows screen recording through the use of overlays.

iOS

Doceri [trial/paid] combines screencasting, desktop control, and an interactive whiteboard in one application, with control through Airplay or through Mac or PC.

Educreations Interactive Whiteboard [free] is an interactive whiteboard and screencasting tool that allows annotation, animation, and narration of a number of content types.

Screenchomp [free] allows users to annotate pictures or to use the application as a whiteboard. Any work completed with the application can be saved automatically to the internet.

Computer

ilos screen recorder [free] automatically uploads content to their servers for storage and playback.

Screencast-O-Matic [free] offers fifteen minutes of recording time for free, both for screen and webcam, and allows users to save to places such as YouTube or as a video file.

TechSmith Camtasia Studio [free trial] is a comprehensive screen recording application that allows for audio and webcam capture as well as highlighting, adding media, and editing of recordings.

Web – n/a

Storyboarding and Scripting

Android

Ray Story Board [free] is a simple storyboard creator that lets users build storyboards from photos or gallery images, create multiple storyboards, and animate them using a slideshow feature.

Storyboard Studio [paid] is a mobile storyboarding writing tool that is suitable for artists and non-artists alike.

iOS

Penultimate [free] provides a natural feel of writing and sketching on paper, and connects to Evernote.

Storyboard Composer [paid] is a mobile storyboard previsualiztion composer for animators, art directors, film students, film directors, or anyone who would like to visualize their story.

Computer

FrameForge Previz Studio [paid] allows users to develop and previsualize films, TV shows, commercials, or similar projects at a professional level.

Storyboardpro [paid] is professional level software that combines drawing and animation tools with camera controls.

StoryBoard Quick Studio [paid] allows for the fast creation of storyboards with QuickShots, has a print-to-sketch feature, and comes with a series of character poses for integration into storylines.

Web

Google Docs [free] can be used, along with any note-taking or document editor, as a make-shift storyboard by integrating photos or pictures into the document to outline a process or the actions for a story. It is also available as an Android and iOS app.

StoryboardThat [free trial] offers an edition that allows educators to build diagrams, and visualize workflow. It features a drag and drop interface and an extensive image library.

Story Creation Apps
Android

StoryMaker 1 [free] provides a means of creating stories using templates and overlays, and the possibility of using audio, photos, or video.

Storehouse [free] allows users to share a collection of photos in a collage or album, or by telling a story that links the photos.

iOS

StoryKit [free] allows for the creation of an electronic storybook through the use of images, simple drawings, recording of sound, and by the addition of text.

Storyrobe [paid] makes photo-based slideshows with voice recording.

FotoBabble [free] adds audio to a photo to make a talking postcard.

Sock Puppets [free] lets users create lip-synced videos with characters. Various puppets, props, scenery, and backgrounds can be used.

Computer

Cartoon Story Maker 1.1 [free] is a simple program that creates 2D cartoon stories with conversations, dialogs (recorded and/or speech bubble), and various backgrounds.

StoryMaker [free/trial] is game-based software that asks for parts of speech (such as nouns, verbs, adjectives), and these are then inserted into a story with sometimes comical results. Educators can edit and customize aspects of the aspects of the program for their context. Backgrounds can be imported, but character templates are built in.

Web

Littlebirdtales [free] provides younger learners the ability to create digital storybooks.

Pixton [free/paid] is a visual writing tool that allows users to make a comic using images, clipart backgrounds and artwork, as well as speech bubbles.

Storynet.org [free] is a website that aims at connecting people to and through storytelling.

StoryJumper [free] allows users to create illustrated storybooks from scratch or from existing templates.

Video Editing

Android

VideoShow – Video Editor [free] is an all-in-one video editor and slideshow producer that provides music, themes, filters, emojis, as well as text input.

VidTrim [free] is a video editor and organizer that allows the trimming, editing, and saving of videos.

VivaVideo: Free Video Editor [free] is a comprehensive video editor and movie maker that facilitates the creation of video-based stories.

WeVideo [free] is a comprehensive and easy to use video editor that can mix images, text, video, and audio.

iOS

iMovie [paid] is video creation and editing software that can create easily shareable content.

Splice [free] is a video editor that adds music and effects to images and videos with narration. It includes access to free songs, sound effects, text overlays, transitions, filters, and various editing tools.

ReelDirector II [paid] is a full-featured video editing app.

WeVideo [free] is an easy to use and comprehensive video editor that can mix audio, images, text, and audio.

Computer

Windows Movie Maker [free] is a video editing software application that allows for narration, audio, images, and video to be mixed and edited with transitions and special effects.

Web

Video Toolbox [free] is an online video editing and conversion tool.

WeVideo [free] is a comprehensive and easy to use web-based video editor that can mix images, text, video, and audio together to form a compelling story.

Video Resources

Android

TED [free] provides more than 2,000 TED talks from various people by topic and mood, and on a variety of topics.

Vimeo [free] is a variety of videos are available across a wide variety of topics and genres, with users having the ability to upload their own content as well.

YouTube [free] allows for editing and uploading of videos, where one can subscribe to various channels that offer a wide variety of videos on various topics and genres.

iOS

TED [free] provides more than 2,000 TED talks from various people by topic and mood, and on a variety of topics.

Vimeo [free] provides a variety of videos which are available across a wide variety of topics and genres. Users are able to upload their own content as well.

YouTube [free] allows for editing and uploading of videos, where once can subscribe to various channels that offer a wide variety of videos on various topics and genres.

Computer – n/a

Web

Clipcanvas [free] allows for the download of 600,000 royalty free HD and 4K video and film clips.

Mazwai [free] maintains a collection of free to use HD video clips and footage, and some unique time-lapse and slow motion video footages that are provided under the Creative Commons Attribution license if used commercially.

Motion Backgrounds for Free [free] is a place to download professional quality motion backgrounds and video footage.

Motion Elements [free] is a good source for premium stock videos, offering around 400 videos for free, as well as free After Effects templates.

Neo's Clip Archive [free] offers nearly 3,500 free video clips sorted by 25 categories free for use for personal, non-commercial purposes.

Pexels Videos [free] brings under one roof a video library of Creative Commons Zero licensed stock videos from a variety of different sources.

SaveTube [free] allows users to rip YouTube videos to their local computer in various audio or video-based formats.

Savevideo.me [free] allows users to rip videos from a variety of sites to their local computer.

TeacherTube [free] is an online resource that helps users to view and share videos, photos, audio, and documents on almost any topic.

WebQuests

Android – n/a

iOS – n/a

Computer – n/a

Web

Building a WebQuest [free] is a comprehensive overview of the template to follow when there is a need to construct a WebQuest.

Having Fun with Reading [free] is a WebQuest for college and adult level learners of English, where learners interact with texts and complete activities that promote cooperative and collaborative learning along with reading narrative comprehension skills.

Idioms in Your Pocket [free] is a WebQuest that is designed for high school and adult ESL students, and it allows them to discover the various meanings of English idioms.

OneStopEnglish WebQuests [free] provides a selection of WebQuests covering major holidays.

Pre-Writing Your WebQuest [free] provides prompts for users to complete in order to develop a WebQuest.

QuestGarden [free/paid] is a site designed by Bernie Dodge, the creator of WebQuests, for use by pre- and in-service teachers, professional developers, other educators, and those who work with them. The site provides hosting and template creation of WebQuests that then become searchable.

Using WebQuests to Teach English [free] is a WebQuest that can be used to teach teachers about WebQuests.

WebQuestDirect [free] is described as the world's largest searchable directory of WebQuest reviews.

WebQuest.Org [free] provides comprehensive information pertaining to the WebQuest model, and is run by Bernie Dodge, the creator of WebQuests.

Zunal [free/paid] is a site for educators to create, host, and then share their WebQuests with others.

Wikis

Android

EveryWiki: Wikipedia++ [free] aims to provide access to many wikis from a central application.

wikiHow [free] is the application associated with the leading how-to-guide wikiHow. It allows for searching of the wiki to find step-by-step instructions on how to complete almost any task.

iOS

Hack My Life – Life Hack Wiki [free] is an application that seeks to provide access to all possible life hacks. A life hack is a strategy or technique that can be used or adopted to allow for better time management or for getting more out of everyday activities.

Lyrically [free] offers access to a list of song lyrics curated by fans. Searches can be undertaken by track, artist, or by song, and there is support for in-app purchases.

Computer

DokuWiki [free] is a PHP based highly customizable and fully extensible wiki software platform. The advantage is that it requires no databases as all the data is stored in plain text, and for this reason, it is very popular and used by many sites. It has a variety of useful features, from locking to avoid edits through to a spam blacklist.

MediaWiki [free] is open-source and it is the wiki software used by Wikipedia. It is available in a number of languages, released under a general public license (GPL), and written in PHP: Hypertext Preprocessor (PHP) a server-side scripting language. There are many extensions and plugins available for free, including a what-you-see-is-what-you-get (WYSIWYG) editor.

Web

PBworks [free] (formerly PBwiki) is a real-time collaborative editing system with several solutions including one for educators. It offers a single workspace, where student accounts can be created without email addresses, and easy editing without the need for coding.

PmWiki [free] is a wiki tool that gives user-access control over individual pages, so they can be set for access by specific people with it being possible to set different passwords for each page. The software also allows for navigation trails through individual sections, insertion of tables, and provides a printable layout.

Wikidot [free] offers members the ability to create a wiki-based website with forums, where they can create a community, or publish and share documents and content.

Wikispaces [free] is a wiki hosting service that provides educators with a means to monitor student progress in real time and the ability to easily create projects and assign them to students, as well as editing tools and a social newsfeed.

Teacher Notes

Android

_____

_____

_____

_____

_____

_____

_____

_____

_____

_____

_____

_____

_____

_____

_____

_____

_____

_____

_____

_____

_____

iOS

Computer

_____

_____

_____

_____

_____

_____

_____

_____

_____

_____

_____

_____

_____

_____

_____

_____

_____

_____

_____

_____

Web

_____

_____

_____

_____

_____

_____

_____

_____

_____

_____

_____

_____

_____

_____

_____

_____

_____

_____

_____

_____

_____

_____

_____

16

References

Aljehani, W. M. A. (2015). Using Prezi presentation software to enhance vocabulary learning of EFL secondary school students. *Educational Research International, 4*(4). 67-81.

Bruder, P. The toolbox: Prezi presentations engage and motivate students. *NJEA Review, 84*(6), 30-32.

Crosby, C. (2010). Prezi: Shaking off the PowerPoint death grip. *Slaw*. Retrieved from http://www.slaw.ca/2010/10/25/prezi-shaking-off-the-powerpoint-death-grip/

Laurillard, D., Stratfold, M., Luckin, R., Plowman, L., & Taylor, J. (2000). Affordances for learning in a non-linear narrative medium. *Journal of Interactive Media in Education, 2*.

Leberecht, T. (2009, August 23). Power to Prezi! *CNet News*. Retrieved from http://news.cnet.com/8301-13641_3-10315737-44.html

Lechlitner, M., Kocain, M., Reitz, K., Stroman, L., Kwon, I., Sheldon, B., Peedin, I., Chalfant, J., Robinson, C., Siebenhausen, N., Towns, W., Boldebuck, M., Applegate, L., Cain, B., & Cunningham, A. (2011). Prezi. *Web 2.0 tools - New possibilities for teaching and learning*. Retrieved from https://wiki.itap.purdue.edu/display/ INSITE/Prezi

Leimbach, L. (2010). Prezi. Just plain good for content. *Teacher Tech*. Retrieved from http://rsu2 teachertech.wordpress.com/2010/11/09/prezi-just-plain-good-for-content/

Peridore, S. & Lines, C. (2011). An online educational framework for second language teaching. In C. Ho & M. Lin (Eds.), *Proceedings of E-Learn: World Conference on E-Learning in Corporate, Government, Healthcare, and Higher Education* 2011 (pp. 365-368). Chesapeake, VA: Association for the Advancement of Computing in Education (AACE).

Pinto Pires, S. (2010). Prezi killed PowerPoint! How to integrate Prezi in the classroom. *e-blahblah*. Retrieved from http://e-blahblah.com/index.php/2010/01/prezi-killed-powerpoint-how-to-integrate-prezi-in-the-classroom/

Potter, N. (2011). Prezi for the win? Ten top tips to make a good one. *the wikiman*. Retrieved from http://thewikiman.org/blog/?p=866

Rhinehart Neas, L. M. (2012). Assessing with PowerPoint and Prezi presentations. *Bright Hub Education*. Retrieved from http://www.brighthub education.com/student-assessment-tools/59411-powerpoint-presentations-as-assessment-tool/

Robinson, S. (2014). Embracing 21st century literacies in the ELA classroom. In J. Vitelli & M. Leikomaa (Eds.), *Proceedings of Edmedia: World Conference on Educational Media and Technology 2014* (pp. 1811-1825). Association for the Advancement of Computing in Education (AACE).

Sabio, R. (2010). Prezi presentations. *EFL and ESL Lesson Plans*. Retrieved from http://www.ralphsesl junction.com/prezi.html

Schar, S., Schluep, S., Schierz, C., & Krueger, H. (2000). Interaction for computer aided learning. *Interactive Multimedia Electronic Journal of Computer-Enhanced Learning, 2(1)*.

Swinford, E. (2006). *Fixing PowerPoint annoyances: How to fix the most annoying things about your favorite presentation program*. CA: O'Reilly.

Watrall, E. (2009). Challenging the presentation paradigm: Prezi. *ProfHacker. Chronicle of Higher Education*. Retrieved from http://chronicle.com/blogs/profhacker/challenging-the-presentation-paradigm-prezi/22646

About the Book

Every student has, at some point in his or her academic life, been required to give a presentation, and in recent years, class presentations have needed to be tied increasingly to multimedia. It is here where Prezi offers a dynamic means of creating a multimedia-based presentation that can actively engage students, particularly in the smart board context where touch navigation is a key component, and one that allows for carrying out a variety of activities from within the same presentation. Prezi use also promotes active learning, with strengths of the presentation platform providing a unique way to establish interest in key topics, direct attention to various subjects, motivate and engage learners, and draw on the creative talents of students as they start to design and develop their own Prezis. The pedagogical possibilities arising from the use of the Prezi presentation paradigm in the context of teaching English to speakers of other languages (TESOL) are offered, along with an overview of instructional strategies, tasks, and activities suitable for multimedia presentation development with learners. Tutorials on how to get started with Prezi are included, along with photocopiable handouts and templates, evaluation techniques, and a comprehensive resource list.

About the Author

David Kent is an Assistant Professor at the Graduate School of TESOL-MALL at Woosong University in the Republic of Korea. He has been working and teaching in Korea since 1995, and with a Doctorate of Education from Curtin University in Australia, he is a specialist in computer assisted language learning (CALL) and the teaching of English to speakers of other languages (TESOL). He has presented at international conferences, as well as published a number of peer-reviewed journal articles, books, and book chapters in his areas of specialization.

Also by David Kent

A Loanword Approach to the Teaching of
English as a Foreign Language in Korea:
Exploring the Effectiveness of a Multimedia Curriculum

TESOL Strategy Guides
Digital Storytelling
The Prezi Presentation Paradigm

www.ingramcontent.com/pod-product-compliance
Lightning Source LLC
Chambersburg PA
CBHW031548040426
42452CB00006B/242